As For Me And My House

A PRACTICAL GUIDE FOR LEADING YOUR KIDS TO CHRIST

ANITA HOUGHTON

Copyright © 2019 Anita Houghton
Published by Ministry23, LLC
Clayton, NC, 27527
ministry23.com

Scripture texts in this work are taken from the New American Bible, revised edition © 2010, 1991, 1986, 1970 Confraternity of Christian Doctrine, Washington, D.C. and are used by permission of the copyright owner. All Rights Reserved. No part of the New American Bible may be reproduced in any form without permission in writing from the copyright owner.

Book Design: Jeremiah Austin, DeNovo Creative

IMPRIMATUR and NIHIL OBSTAT:
Most Rev. Arturo Cepeda
Censor Librorum
Auxiliary Bishop of Detroit, Michigan, USA
September 4, 2019

Table of Contents

Acknowledgments... iii

Chapter One
What is your dream for your children?............................ 1

Chapter Two
Where do I begin?... 5

Chapter Three
Who is Jesus?.. 9

Chapter Four
Why did Jesus die on the cross?................................ 15

Chapter Five
How do I pass the baton?...................................... 21

Bibliography... 37

Acknowledgments

First, I would like to express gratitude to my parents, Zygmunt and Elwira Czajkowski for all that they have done to hand on the Catholic faith to me. Throughout their lives, they have modeled a deep love for Christ and his Church, steadfast love for one another in good times and in bad, and selfless generosity in helping those who are less fortunate.

Many thanks to Phil Mooney and to my colleagues Michael King and Tara Stenger for reading the book and offering suggestions on how to improve its content and delivery.

I also want to express gratitude to Bishop Arturo Cepeda for reviewing this material for consistency with Magisterial Teaching and granting permission to publish this work.

In addition, I express deep gratitude to my husband Mike, for his input and feedback as well as his encouragement throughout the development of this work.

I dedicate this book to my children Matt, Nick and Melissa who are the joy of my life. May the Lord continue to walk with you, bless you, and fill you with His grace as you pursue your dreams and one day hand on the faith to your own children and grandchildren.

Chapter One

What is your dream for your children?

Train the young in the way they should go;
even when old, they will not swerve from it. (Proverbs 22:6)

What is your dream for your children? When I do presentations for parents whose children are preparing for the sacraments of Reconciliation and Eucharist, I often begin my talk with this question. The answers I commonly receive include health, happiness, a good education, a good career, and good friends, etc. Never once has anyone said "Heaven! My dream for my child is eternal life with God in heaven!" Quite honestly, it's not something that most parents think about, especially in the midst of busy family life. It certainly was not on my radar when I was a young mother. No one had ever told me that this was something that God had entrusted to me. Somehow, I did not connect the dots even though I made the promise that every other Catholic parent makes when bringing a child for baptism:

> Celebrant: You have asked to have your child baptized. In doing so you are accepting the responsibility of training him (her) in the practice of the faith. It will be your duty to bring him (her) up to keep God's commandments as Christ taught us, by loving God and our neighbor. Do you clearly understand what you are undertaking?

I dutifully answered, "I do," but, honestly, I had no idea what that entailed.

In retrospect, it would have been helpful if someone had taken the time to help me reflect on what it really means to raise my child in the faith and to help me to anticipate the challenges and obstacles that would come my way in doing so. It would have also been helpful to get some dos and don'ts from parents who have traveled this road before me.

However, as I matured in my own faith, my role in raising my children in the faith became increasingly clear. Over time, I came to realize that I, as a Catholic parent, have the awesome privilege and responsibility to help my children come to know Jesus and to help them discover God's plan for their lives. I also have the responsibility to help them recognize that the real purpose of their lives in this world is to *work out their salvation for the next*. As I began to internalize this idea, the faith life of my children became my No. 1 priority. I realized that there are many important things that I can do for my kids—encourage them to do well in school, give them opportunities to explore their gifts and talents, help them to gain proficiency in these skills so they can be competitive in the world, help them to be responsible citizens and to make good choices. But while all of these are really good things to do, in the end, they are short-term goals. Faith is the best legacy I can pass on to my children. It is the only thing that's truly important since it is what gives ultimate meaning to our lives and helps to direct us to our ultimate end. Perhaps one of the reasons that I was driven to this conclusion was the sudden loss of two close people in my life within a three-month period. Both of these individuals died young, and it was a wake-up call that helped me to realize that this life is short, eternity is long, and the Christian life is about living with our *ultimate* end in mind. God had my attention, and he began the work of transforming my life.

One of the many fruits that came from this transformation was a new-found appreciation for how powerfully family life can impact the faith trajectory of my children. Families are close to God's heart. In fact, they were his idea in the first place. God has given the human family great dignity and purpose—to raise up children who know him, love him, and walk in his ways.

Deuteronomy 6 reminds us that parents are called to cultivate in their children a love for God above all else:

> Hear, O Israel! The LORD is our God, the LORD alone! Therefore, you shall love the LORD, your God, with your whole heart, and with your whole being, and with your whole strength. Take to heart these words which I command you today. Keep repeating them to your children. Recite them when you are at home and when you are away, when you lie down and when you get up. Bind them on your arm as a sign and let them be as a pendant on your forehead. Write them on the doorposts of your houses and on your gates. (Deuteronomy 6:6-8)

God is calling parents in no uncertain terms to ensure that the love of God takes root in the hearts of their children, and no human community is better equipped to do this than the family. It is the perfect "small group" where faith is lived out in real and tangible ways. While everyday life in the family may seem filled with a lot of ordinariness and at times a lot of chaos, it provides countless opportunities to respond in the way Jesus would. It might be forgiving your spouse, asking for God's help in making a tough decision, having a difficult heart-to-heart talk with your teenager, or praying with your child before a big day at school. Seen in this light, the "ordinary" life of a family becomes quite extraordinary indeed.

I also discovered that God never gives a mission without providing the means needed to carry it out. God does not expect me to do all this on my own power. Rather, he wants me to be dependent on him so that he can provide me the grace and wisdom to be a good wife and mother and help me during the challenging moments of family life.

What role do you want God to play in the life of your children when they are adults? Do you want faith to be a powerful force that supports them in their challenges and fears? Do you want faith to ground their moral compass? Do you want your children to have hope in a world that's filled with despair? Do you want their faith in God to be strong enough so that they have the fortitude to raise their own children in the faith? Many parents want to make a difference in the faith lives of their children but aren't sure how to start. Sometimes it can be like trying to navigate a road without a GPS. That's why I wrote this book—to offer some friendly advice from someone who has traveled this road, even though I've hit a few bumps and taken a few wrong turns along the way.

Children today face more challenges than ever... and at a younger age. While social media has many positive aspects, it also has numerous negative effects on children. Photoshopped images set an unattainable standard for what their bodies should look like. Cyberbullying and the illusion that everyone has a perfect life can leave them with a sense of inadequacy. It's not surprising that anxiety and depression among youth are on the rise. In addition, in an increasingly globalized and interconnected world, our children are exposed to and greatly influenced by secular worldviews and nonbiblical perspectives. There was a time—fifty or sixty years ago—when the culture was more visibly Christian and church affiliation was socially acceptable. Today that is not the case. The best way to equip your children to face these challenges and to cultivate in them a Christian worldview is to help them to meet Jesus and grow in relationship with him and his Church.

You want the best for your kids, but our heavenly Father wants this more than you do! It's comforting to know that you don't have to be an expert to raise your kids in the faith. God does not expect us to be perfect; he just asks us to be faithful. God will send his Holy Spirit to be your GPS, and he will guide you if you but open your heart to receive the grace for the journey.

Questions for Individual Reflection or Small Group Discussion

1. What strikes you about the passage from Deuteronomy 6?
2. What role do you want God to play in the life of your children when they are adults?
3. What challenges do today's parents face in handing on the faith to their kids?

Chapter Two

Where do I begin?

*Trust in the LORD with all your heart,
on your own intelligence do not rely;
In all your ways be mindful of him,
and he will make straight your paths. (Proverbs 3:5-6)*

When my kids were little, I had the privilege of serving as a catechist at my parish. My experience as a catechist and then later as a Director of Religious Education, and a diocesan leader convinced me that something more was needed in the process of faith formation to help children make their faith real. Year after year, I witnessed children completing their lessons and receiving the sacraments, without any visible sign that Jesus was a real part of their lives. It was like pouring water on a rock; nothing seemed to stick. My experience is not uncommon, as I meet regularly with other church leaders whose experience is similar to mine. It is sobering to realize that this dynamic has been in play for decades.

As Catholics, our parish faith formation programs are accustomed to focusing on teaching doctrine in a systematic way in order to help children grow into the fullness of Christian life. This is important, but it doesn't come first. Children (as well as adults) are ready to receive the teachings of the Church *only after* they've encountered Jesus, fallen in love with him, and responded to him in faith. Think about a time when you were madly in love with someone. Falling in love affects you psychologically and behaviorally. It leaves you with feelings of euphoria, it makes you smile when you're alone, and it makes you do all kinds of things that are out of your comfort zone. The person you love occupies your mind from the moment you wake up to the moment you fall asleep, and you do everything you can to know that person more deeply and grow in relationship. The same is true for Jesus. Encountering Jesus is life-changing; it transforms your desires and your priorities.

The idea that evangelization (helping someone encounter Jesus and respond to him in faith) precedes catechesis (the systematic teaching of doctrine) was not on my radar when I was a young mother and a volunteer catechist at my parish. In addition, I didn't realize that catechesis *presumes* that the child is already evangelized and that all of the textbooks used in these programs are written from this vantage point. It's no wonder that many of the kids in my catechism class weren't really interested in what I was teaching! They had never encountered Jesus and my teaching was falling on deaf ears.

I share this background to make the following two points: 1) Although some parishes and Catholic schools have begun incorporating evangelization into their religion curriculum, they alone can't lead your children to Jesus. *You* are the secret sauce to the whole endeavor. What you can provide in a family setting is irreplaceable and incapable of being entirely delegated to others, and 2) When you embark on the journey of faith with your children, it's important to help them meet Jesus first before teaching them the doctrines of the Church. I wasn't aware of the importance of doing this when my kids were little, and I believe that their faith would have taken root more deeply had I done so. If you're not sure that you know Jesus well enough to introduce him to your children (or the teachings of the Church for that matter), I have great news for you: you can learn along with them. You don't have to have it all figured out ahead of time. Jesus is a great teacher; he will lead you and send the Holy Spirit to guide your every step.

Many people don't know that you can actually have a loving, intimate relationship with Jesus. You might be thinking, "Is that really a thing?" Yes, it's really a thing. God isn't just a force, spiraling in the universe. God is a communion of Persons, Father, Son and Holy Spirit. God the Father sent his Son, Jesus into the world so that we would know him, love him, and be saved by him.

"A journey of a thousand miles begins with a single step." This saying teaches that even the longest and most difficult ventures have a starting point, something which begins with one first step. I suggest that the first step in the next phase of your family's faith journey is getting to know Jesus more intimately.

Questions for Individual Reflection or Small Group Discussion

1. Think of the first time you fell in love. How did that affect or change you?
2. Do you believe that an intimate relationship with Jesus is possible? Why or why not?
3. Who is Jesus to you?

Chapter Three

Who is Jesus?

For when peaceful stillness encompassed everything and the night in its swift course was half spent, Your all-powerful word from heaven's royal throne leapt into the doomed land. (Wisdom 18:14-15)

Several years ago, I did a presentation for a group of parents and showed a video titled *Who Was Jesus?* The video was a compilation of responses from street interviews of young adults who were asked the question, "Who was Jesus?" While a few of the respondents were able to describe who Jesus was, many others floundered:

> "He was born, and he became this like a prophet for eventually what would become Christianity."

> "I don't really have an opinion on Jesus; I believe that religion was just created to control the masses really."

> "I think he is a pretty cool guy; he had a peaceful philosophy; I think he's misinterpreted by a lot of people."

> "I don't know because I don't really believe in him so I don't think anything about him."

> "He could be a real person I'm sure he was, I mean, I'm sure he was just, you know, good at what he did or something."

"I feel that Jesus is a modern-day scapegoat."

"Jesus is God, I think."

"Jesus was a man from what I figure."

"He was a dude from back in the day, pretty awesome; he had a beard."

"He probably existed, but I don't believe that he was the Son of God."

Many people don't know much about Jesus. In recent decades, there has been a significant decline in the Church's influence over society. Christianity is giving way to a secularist worldview under which more and more people are seeing religious faith and morality as not only optional and outdated but even disagreeable. As a result, much of the culture has closed itself off to Christ. These video responses reflect that.

So, who is Jesus, really? Let's start at the beginning. God is a communion of Persons: Father, Son, and Holy Spirit. God is eternal. Since humans measure everything in time, it is very hard for us to conceive of someone who had no beginning, but has always been, and will continue forever. Our brains also struggle to comprehend God's power and majesty. Next time you look up at the stars on a clear night and ponder the vastness of the universe, consider that God created it all! Next time you're standing on the beach overlooking the ocean, consider the millions of species of life that team in the waters. God created all of these too. The created world reveals to us God's beauty, glory, power, wisdom, presence, creativity, and most of all, his loving care. The Bible reveals to us that God didn't just create our world and leave us to our own devices. God enters into history and chooses to reveal himself to us and make known to us his will for our lives: to share in his own blessed life. He does this in a particular way through Jesus.

At the appointed time, God sent his Son Jesus into the world. Jesus was conceived in the womb of his mother Mary through the power of the Holy Spirit. You might be wondering… how could a God who is without limits become a microscopic speck inside Mary's womb? The most honest answer is this: We don't know because what happened was a miracle of the highest order. No man was involved in the process. Not Joseph. Not a Roman soldier. Not any other man. The virginal conception of Jesus was a direct creative act of God and is a mystery we will never fully understand. Unlike every other human whose life begins at conception, technically, Jesus' life did not begin at his conception. Jesus, the Second Person of the Trinity, is eternal and has existed forever with God the Father and God the Holy Spirit. At a point in human history, "he came down from heaven, and by the Holy Spirit was incarnate of the Virgin Mary," as we profess in the Nicene Creed every Sunday at Mass. This helps us to better understand who Jesus is. Jesus is not just a prophet, a great teacher, a martyr who died for a great cause, a revolutionary who started a religion, or a pretty cool guy with a peaceful philosophy. He is the incarnate Son of God. Christianity is unique among world religions because it's more than just a set of moral teachings and a way of life; it hinges on the identity of Jesus, who is fully God and fully man.

For the first thirty years of his life, Jesus lived like any other person. He lived in Nazareth which is in the northern part of Israel about one hundred miles north of Jerusalem. The Bible doesn't give us too many insights into this part of Jesus' life, but from what we do know Jesus displayed extraordinary wisdom and knowledge as a youth.

Jesus' public ministry began when he was thirty years old with his baptism in the Jordan River. Upon coming out of the water, the heavens were opened, the Spirit of God descended upon him like a dove, and a voice came from heaven saying, "This is my beloved Son, with whom I am well pleased." (Matthew 3:16-17) Jesus was then driven by the Spirit to the desert for forty days and forty nights to be tempted by the devil. After resisting these temptations, the devil left him, and he began his ministry in Galilee. He chose twelve apostles who traveled with him throughout the country, and he began to teach and proclaim the kingdom of God. Jesus was anointed with the Holy Spirit and with power, and people couldn't get enough of him. He taught with authority and conviction. People were astonished at his mighty works; he made the lame walk, the blind see, the deaf hear, and he raised people from the dead. The people marveled, "Who is this man?" "We've never seen anything like this!" The news of Jesus spread throughout the land and wherever he went, crowds followed him, bringing the sick and those possessed by demons.

At the time of Jesus, Judea was occupied and governed by the Roman Empire. This time period was filled with political, socioeconomic, and religious tension. Jesus caused controversy among the leaders of the day in a number of ways. Jesus outraged the Jewish religious leaders because he pointed out their hypocrisy, pride, and arrogance. Jesus ignored the religious traditions they observed so minutely because he knew they were man-made rules that had not come from God; this infuriated the religious leaders! Jesus was a threat to their religious system because more and more people began to believe in him and follow him. The Jewish religious leaders sought to kill him because Jesus claimed equality with God. For the Romans, he was a political threat who was causing unrest in the region. A few high-ranking Jewish authorities conspired with Roman leaders to have Jesus put to death; the charge was blasphemy—the claim that he was God. As a result, Jesus was crucified just like many other prophets and rebels during the first century.

The most amazing part of the story of Jesus in his resurrection. On the third day after his death, Jesus rose from the dead. The main reason Jesus' disciples believed in the resurrection was that they saw him alive after he was dead! Jesus presented himself to many of his followers on a number of different occasions. You can imagine their initial hesitation and the astonishment at seeing him. They could not ignore the fact that he was alive and that it was really him! However, Jesus did not return to a normal human life after his resurrection. Jesus' resurrected body was different than it was before; he was not merely a resuscitated corpse. He had a new kind of existence that did not belong to the realm of this world. He had a physical body that did not obey physical laws. The Bible tells us that he appeared out of nowhere and vanished from sight, yet he ate and drank proving to his disciples that he was not a ghost but had a real body. Jesus was living *anew* in the power of God.

Forty days after his resurrection, Jesus ascended to heaven both visibly and bodily. Before ascending to heaven, Jesus gave his final instructions to his disciples:

> All power in heaven and on earth has been given to me. Go, therefore, and make disciples of all nations, baptizing them in the name of the Father, and of the Son, and of the Holy Spirit, teaching them to observe all that I have commanded you. And behold, I am with you always, until the end of the age. (Matthew 28:18-20)

Before his passion, death, and resurrection, Jesus prepared his disciples for a time that he would no longer be with them in a physical sense. Jesus promised that he would send them the Holy Spirit to teach them and remind them of everything that he taught. Jesus delivered on his promise ten days after he ascended into heaven. When the Holy Spirit fell upon the disciples, they were not only filled with courage and strength for the mission, they were also given spiritual gifts to be used for the sake of others to continue the work that Jesus began in his earthly ministry. Just like Jesus, the disciples proclaimed God's plan of salvation, healed the sick, and even raised the dead. These miracles were met with wonder and awe, and more importantly, faith in Jesus. The disciples met the Son of God, and with the power they received from him, they were able to convince the world of who he is and what he accomplished through his passion, death, and resurrection.

The question posed to the young adults in the video speaks of Jesus in the past tense: "Who *was* Jesus?" The question should have been, "Who *is* Jesus?" It's important to remember that Jesus is not dead and gone, but very much alive today. He continues to live his new existence in his glorified, resurrected body. In his earthly life, Jesus' human body was subject to death, but because Jesus has been raised from the dead, *death has no more power over him*. Jesus has conquered death and forever wedded himself to the human race so that we too might not be subject to the power of death but have the gift of eternal life.

Questions for Individual Reflection or Small Group Discussion

1. What aspect of Jesus' life is most captivating to you?
2. How have you witnessed Jesus at work in your life (i.e., answered prayers, miracles, etc.)?
3. What do you think Jesus meant when he said, "Go and make disciples of all nations?"
4. What would it have been like to witness the apostles doing mighty works by the power of the Holy Spirit?

Chapter Four

Why did Jesus die on the cross?

*For the wages of sin is death,
but the gift of God is eternal life in Christ Jesus our Lord. (Romans 6:23)*

A crucifix is usually the first thing you see when you enter a Catholic church. We hang them on the walls of our homes and in our Catholic schools and universities. Modern-day fashion has turned the cross into a fad where people gladly wear it on their shirts, pants, and on their bodies as either jewelry or tattoo art. Some wear it proudly to show off their style, while others wear it humbly as an expression of their faith. In first-century Palestine, we wouldn't see anyone parading around with crosses around their necks. In fact, the only people we would see bearing crosses would be criminals who were marching to their death. To first-century Romans, the cross was something that was feared, not admired; it meant death, not life.

How did an instrument of torture become the means of our salvation? What was accomplished by Jesus' death on the cross? When we say, "Jesus died for our sins," what does that really mean? The answers to these questions not only help us understand the deeper meaning and purpose of Jesus' life but also why Jesus is relevant to us today. Many people who've been raised Catholic, received religious education and received the sacraments know that a Savior exists, but few understand why we *need* a Savior. In order to better grasp this, we need to first take a few steps back to understand God's personal love for each one of us, the consequences of sin, and how and why God intervened on our behalf.

In the beginning, God created everything out of nothing, and he created it out of love. He created the universe, our planet, all the plants and animals, and at the crown of his creation he created human beings. God created human beings that they might share in his own divine life for all eternity. When Jesus hung on the cross, he cried, "I Thirst." This was not a mere physical thirst, as we might think. Thirst is a metaphor for "desire." God thirsts for each person he's ever created. Jesus thirsts for you. He wants to be in a relationship with you, and he thirsts for your love. With over seven billion people on the planet earth, it might be hard to believe that Jesus knows you and loves you personally, but it's true! Jesus knows everything about you… your family, your friends, and your problems. He knows your hopes and dreams, your fears, and what makes you happy. Everything in your life matters to him. Jesus delights in you and has a plan for your life.

God sent his Son, Jesus, into the world to deal with the problem of sin. Sin is a thought, word or action that we freely do, even though we know it's wrong. There are many different ways to sin, but one thing is true of all sin: it has bad consequences. It always hurts our relationships with each other and it hurts our relationship with God. Today, we live in a culture that shrugs off sin. If sin doesn't matter, then we don't really need a Savior. If this is the prevailing attitude, then it should be no surprise that people are indifferent toward Jesus. But God does not shrug off sin; sin has consequences and those consequences can be eternal.

These consequences are revealed to us in the opening chapters of the Bible in the book of Genesis. This part of the Bible uses stories to reveal deep truths about God and man. The story of Adam and Eve helps us to understand the seriousness of sin. Sin came into the world, when our first parents, Adam and Eve, chose to disobey God and eat from the tree from which God forbid them to eat. Adam and Eve didn't trust God and took advantage of their freedom. Instead, they listened to the serpent who tricked them into thinking that eating the fruit would give them the same knowledge as God.

Before sin entered the world, Adam and Eve lived in the garden, a place where they enjoyed pure happiness. (This garden symbolizes heaven.) It was God's plan for them to live like this forever; but when they disobeyed God, He expelled them from the garden. Why? Because God is holy, and nothing that is sinful or unholy can be in God's presence. Paradise (heaven) was lost, not just for Adam and Eve, but for the rest of humanity. This means that because of sin, the eternal life that we are meant for is no longer possible.

Since everyone sins, you might be wondering how anyone can get to heaven. As soon as Adam and Eve sinned, God began his rescue mission. In the Old Testament, we learn that God entered into a covenant with his people, Israel. Through the Jewish people, God would send a Savior to deal with sin once and for all. At the appointed time, Jesus came into the world to offer his life on the cross to take the punishment for all our sins. Our best efforts cannot restore what is lost by sin, but Jesus pays the price on our behalf. That's why we call him our Savior.

God sent his Son, Jesus, into the world to save you. Jesus took all your sins upon himself and offered his life on the cross. As a result, Jesus' death and resurrection opens the gates of heaven to you and to all people. His sacrifice is the solution to the problem of sin.

An analogy might help to make this clear. A man is sentenced to 20 years in prison for a crime that he committed. Just as the judge delivers the sentence, another man in the courtroom stands up and offers to go to prison on his behalf. The judge agrees and the criminal is set free. This extraordinary sacrifice, quite literally, gives the criminal his life back. In a similar way, Jesus sets you free. Through his death and resurrection, Jesus pays the debt for your sins and gives you the gift of eternal life. Even though Jesus suffered, he did this with great love, because he knew that you could never reach heaven without it.

The world is plagued with sin; the number of sins committed is so great that it's impossible to count. A mere man could never redeem all of humanity, but Jesus isn't just a man, he is God. It requires someone infinite and eternal to take on this multitude of sins. With his arms outstretched on the cross, he reaches infinitely into the past and infinitely into the future to save all people of all time, including you.

The whole life of the Church, most especially the sacraments, draws its power from what Jesus accomplished on the cross. Jesus is the source of life now and forever. What he did for us on the cross changed the course of human history. If it wasn't for Jesus, there would be no heaven. While Adam and Eve set the course for death and destruction, Jesus set a course for life and restoration. But, the cross isn't an automatic ticket to heaven! We have to respond to Jesus' offer of salvation by making a choice to follow him.

Here's another analogy to help understand what is meant by "response." Imagine for a moment that you had a friend who literally saved your life— you were about to get hit by a train and he pushed you out of the way just in time for both of you to be safe. Now, imagine the next time you saw this friend. Would you just give him a fist-bump and go back to things like normal? Or would you be thinking of a million different ways you could do or say something to thank him for what he did? Would you ever see this person in the same way, knowing that because of him you are still alive? Similarly, think of all that God has done for you and everyone you love! Jesus crushes death (the thing we are most afraid of) and offers us eternal life! God deserves to be praised! The worst thing we could do is forget—forget who he is, forget what he's done, and forget the incredible life that he's called us to.

In the Gospel of John, Jesus stands up and exclaims, "Let anyone who thirsts come to me and drink." (John 7:37) But notice that this invitation is specifically addressed to those who are thirsty. Before we can really have a close relationship with God, we have to thirst for God. The problem is, not too many people are thirsting for him. In fact, many people are simply indifferent. This indifference isn't something that comes at the end of a long inner struggle; it just happens because people simply don't know the possibilities of a life in Christ. Somehow in Catholic circles, many of us have come to believe that our faith is "private" and shouldn't be shared. But nothing could be further from the truth! We need to share with the world the wonderful things that God has accomplished for us and the reason for our hope and joy. Real stories about real people are inspiring and these are ways a dormant desire for God can be stirred into flame, especially for our kids.

Questions for Individual Reflection or Small Group Discussion

1. Look up and read Isaiah 49:15-16a. Pause and in silence listen to what God wants to speak into your heart. What did you hear him say?
2. Why is Jesus of such great significance to the human race?
3. How does it make you feel to know that Jesus died on the cross for *you*?

Chapter Five

How do I pass the baton?

As for me and my house, we will serve the Lord. (Joshua 24:15)

In the Bible, the second letter to Timothy offers a picture of St. Paul at the end of his ministry just before his death. In the closing chapter, St. Paul exhorts Timothy:

> I charge you in the presence of God and of Christ Jesus, who will judge the living and the dead, and by his appearing and his kingly power: proclaim the word; be persistent whether it is convenient or inconvenient; convince, reprimand, encourage through all patience and teaching. For the time will come when people will not tolerate sound doctrine but, following their own desires and insatiable curiosity, will accumulate teachers and will stop listening to the truth and will be diverted to myths. But you, be self-possessed in all circumstances; put up with hardship; perform the work of an evangelist; fulfill your ministry. (2 Timothy 4:1-5)

Timothy is an associate of St. Paul in the ministry to the Gentiles. We can think of St. Paul as a mentor to Timothy and, in many ways, 2 Timothy, reads like a last will and testament. It is a moving account of how Paul, like a runner crossing the finish line, has reached the end of his apostolic career. Paul, after teaching Timothy for more than 15 years, is now passing the baton and instructing him to continue his ministry of preaching. Knowing that death is at his doorstep, Paul hurriedly sends the letter filled with fatherly wisdom and warnings to prepare Timothy for the struggles ahead. The time will come when Timothy himself will pass the baton to others who will teach and defend the gospel for future generations.

In a track and field relay race, there are several key elements to secure a smooth baton handoff. It is the responsibility of the incoming runner to place the baton in the hand of the outgoing runner. The outgoing runner must reach out and keep the hand steady. It is the incoming runner's job to put the baton in the right place. Both have to be moving. Both have to stay in their lane.

This is true also in the Christian life. Like the outbound runner, we ourselves must be open to receive the faith from those that God has sent to us. We need to be in the right stance and running at the right pace in order to receive Jesus and the teachings of the Church. If we are standing still in our spiritual lives, the handoff will be awkward at best. Our hearts have to be open to receive. If we let go of what we've received or left the designated path (i.e. choose to follow false teaching or habitually commit serious sin), we risk being disqualified.

As the race continues, the outbound runner eventually becomes the inbound runner. In this role, it is our duty to tell our children about Jesus and help them to see that we are all in the race and running toward the finish line, which is God himself. If the handoff doesn't happen, the whole team loses. In the 2008 Summer Olympics in Beijing, both the men's and women's 4 x 100 relay teams dropped the baton disqualifying them from the event. I remember thinking how disappointed these athletes must have been to go all the way to the Olympics, only to be disqualified from the race. However, the stakes of the Christian life are far higher than any sporting event. To be disqualified from this race is to forfeit heaven itself.

The good news of Jesus that has been handed on to you must now be handed on to your children so that they, in turn, can hand it on to their children and so on. A good relay team practices handoffs and learns techniques and strategies for being successful. So, what does it take to make a successful handoff of the faith to your children? As you may surmise, there is no silver bullet or secret formula for success. However, there are things that you and your family can do to create an environment of encounter with Christ in your home and strategies that can be employed to nurture faith in your children. I suggest three things for a successful handoff: 1) Strengthen your own spiritual life, 2) Strengthen and nurture your marriage, 3) Make Jesus the center of your home life.

Your Spiritual Life

A 2012 study looked at how parents helped their overweight kids. Some parents changed their kids' diets, while others took their kids to clinics and camps. But the kids who lost the most weight were those whose parents had lost weight themselves. The kids were inspired by their parents' physical activity.[1] The same is true for faith life. Parents are the ultimate role models for kids. Just as airline safety instructions tell us to put on our own oxygen mask before assisting others so parents need to have a living relationship with Jesus and to learn the faith themselves in order to hand it on effectively to their children. Do you realize how much Jesus loves you? Do you realize that he cares about everything that is going on in your life? Do you want to encounter him more deeply?

Encounters with Christ have a life-changing effect on an individual. The Scriptures give us numerous examples. St. Paul's entire life can be explained in terms of his encounter with the risen Christ on the road to Damascus. In an instant, he saw the sin of his former life; he repented and harnessed all of his zeal and energy for one goal—to be an instrument to help others come to know Christ. After encountering the love and mercy of Jesus, the Samaritan woman at the well became an evangelist proclaiming Christ to all who would listen. The leper who encountered Jesus and his healing power was set free from his infirmities. Jesus gave him a new life! He returned home—to be loved and to be alive like never before!

It is no different for us. When we encounter Christ, we experience love beyond our comprehension. In light of Christ, we are able to see our own sins and are inspired to harness our energy to serve Christ and his

---

[1] "Parents Should Lead By Example in Weight Loss, Study Finds," *US News and World Report*, accessed August 3, 2019, https://health.usnews.com/health-news/news/articles/2012/03/22/parents-should-lead-by-example-in-weight-loss-study-finds.

Church. An encounter with Christ gives us a new lease on life; we are healed, restored and forgiven.

An encounter with Christ can be a surprise! Jesus has his own plan for our lives and it is usually different from (and better than) ours. We expect him to give us answers to certain questions, but instead he just gives us more of himself. We expect him to guide us along a certain path in our lives; instead he reminds us that if we seek him first, everything else will follow. We expect him to take away certain sorrows or troubles, but instead he tells us to trust him and wait patiently. Jesus often answers the questions we don't know we need answered. Jesus likes to surprise us and remind us that he's got things under control. So when we encounter him, we should expect the unexpected!

When we encounter Christ we observe the following changes in our lives: a change in our priorities and conversation and a desire to share our experiences with others. We are compelled to reach out to our children, friends, and neighbors, to invite them to meet Jesus and experience the new life that we have experienced. The Scriptures come alive. The sacramental life of the Church has new-found depth and meaning. The experience of God's personal love becomes a new anchor in our lives which enables us to meet challenges and suffering with hope and confidence. It is a realization that there is a new power at work in our lives—the power of the Holy Spirit—which enables us to conquer fear and sin.

Encounters with Jesus rarely happen randomly. Because the world is full of distractions, most often, encounters with Jesus require effort and intentionality. The modern world in which we live is filled with busy schedules and instantaneous communication. The momentum of life discourages us from stopping and taking time to consider Jesus; even if we do, the noise and busyness makes it difficult to be quiet and still so that we can hear his voice.

Every one of us encounters Jesus in different ways. Some of us are hardwired to find Jesus in interactions with other people, while others best connect with Jesus in the privacy of solitude. Many of us encounter Jesus in praying with Sacred Scripture, while others meet Jesus by using their hands and gifts to actively serve others. The bottom line is that there is no limit to the number of ways in which Jesus reveals himself to his beloved. An encounter with Christ can happen in a slow and gradual way, or it can happen suddenly in a dramatic way.

Our disposition is a significant factor in the encounter with Christ being transformative. Jesus respects our free will; he doesn't force himself on us. Because an encounter is about meeting a person, the Person of Jesus Christ, it is not achieved by accumulation of knowledge. Encounter involves trust and surrender. It also involves curiosity and a desire to know him more—an opening of the heart to meet him. The culture in which we live promotes independence, but Jesus wants us to be completely dependent on him. He wants us to be like little children, stripped of our doubts, full of wide-eyed inspiration that comes from total faith. Those who are indifferent, cynical, proud, or antagonistic toward the faith can block themselves from experiencing Christ's presence and his love. On the other hand, those who approach Jesus in humility, faith, and receptivity, find him. "God opposes the proud but bestows favor on the humble." (1 Peter 5:5)

The best way to encounter Christ is to simply ask, "Lord, help me to know that you are real! Reveal yourself to me. Help me to encounter you in a real and tangible way." Jesus tells us to ask and assures us of a favorable response:

> Ask and it will be given to you; seek and you will find; knock and the door will be opened to you. For everyone who asks, receives; and the one who seeks, finds; and to the one who knocks, the door will be opened. (Matthew 7:7-8)

The following are some suggestions to help jump start your spiritual life:

- **Reflect on where you are with the Lord.** Are you close, distant, angry, indifferent, or at peace? Wherever you are, bring it to prayer and talk to God about it.

- **Commit (or recommit) to having a regular prayer life.** A good place to begin is to set aside ten to fifteen minutes per day to be still and be with Jesus. Most people have a hard time sustaining a regular prayer life, so you have to make a decision to just do it. Set a reminder on your phone, write it in your calendar, or do what you need to do to block out the time. Be sure to find a quiet place and turn off your phone. If your home is full of noise, try to find a nearby church or an outdoor space where you can pray. Over time, you will look forward to this oasis of peace and will desire to increase your time with God.
- **Get a Bible** (I suggest NABRE or NRSV-CE translations) and a journal. Use your Bible during your prayer time and write down any inspirations or words you hear from the Lord. Lectio divina (Latin: divine reading) is an ancient technique for meditating on Scripture. Instructions on how to do lectio divina are easily searchable on the Internet. Give it a try!
- **Take advantage of encounter opportunities at your parish** (i.e. Mass, Alpha Course, Eucharistic Adoration, Praise & Worship, Scripture Studies, etc.). These types of programs and events create an environment that opens hearts and creates an environment where Christ can be encountered.
- **Get connected to a small group to be able to share your faith journey with other adults.** There are numerous benefits to being a part of a community of other disciples including making friends who share your values and support you on the journey.
- **Resolve any personal issues you may have.** If you struggle with anxiety, depression, or addiction, get help! God wants to heal you, and once he does, you will have more freedom to serve others. You may begin by talking to a priest or pastoral minister who can then refer you on as needed.

Your Marriage

A healthy marriage is good for you and your children and serves as a solid foundation for family faith life. In God's plan, this is the ideal;

however, over the past twenty years single-parent families have become even more common than a family consisting of a mother, father and children. Today we see all sorts of single parent families: headed by mothers, headed by fathers, headed by a grandparent raising their grandchildren, etc. The good news is that God can be the center of all families, regardless of their size or make-up.

For those who are married, your marriage needs to take priority over work and your kids. This sounds like a no-brainer, but it's so easy to let your spouse take the backseat when you're worn out from caring for kids all day. Similarly, some men and women can get so wrapped up in their work and future ambitions that they have little time for their spouses. But the best gift you can give to your marriage—and to your children—is to love your spouse and to put him or her first. Healthy marriages take a lot of sacrifice. Jesus presents us with a paradox: those intent on saving their lives will lose them; only those who deny themselves will really find themselves. Although marriage is about intimacy and mutual fulfilment of spouses, that will come only when spouses die to themselves so as to serve each other and the children. In addition, when their parents love each other and frequently show that love, it helps kids to feel more loved and secure.

Marriage is intricately bound up in faith life. The human family is like a church in microcosm (we call this the "domestic church"), a place where faith is nurtured and discipleship is lived out in real and tangible ways. Within the walls of the domestic church, children learn about their faith through their parents' word and example. It is within the domestic church that Catholic parents lay out a curriculum of love and forgiveness while helping the family to work out their salvation in the give-and-take of life in the family. A healthy Christian home is an oasis of refreshment for guests who are weary from the pressures and tensions of our modern culture. Families who love God and love one another, who share meals together and truly listen and speak to one another, and do so joyfully are an attractive witness pointing to Christ and his Church.

The following are some suggestions on how to strengthen your marriage:

- **Learn how to pray together.** Every time you and your spouse pray separately for one another, great things happen in your relationship, but when you pray together, that power increases tremendously, and so do the results. Going to God in prayer as a couple benefits your marriage in several ways: it promotes unity, emotional intimacy, and invites God into your relationship. Before you pray together be sure to talk about how you want to go about it and start where you are both comfortable.

- **Go on dates and mini vacations together.** Carving out some time for yourselves away from the stresses of daily life strengthens communication and allows for more intimate conversation. Planning novel experiences can help change up the routine and increase intimacy.

- **Navigate religious differences gently.** Religious differences between spouses can cause tremendous stress on a marriage when one spouse has a devout faith and the other spouse doesn't or when one spouse comes from a different faith tradition. In that situation, both spouses are operating from two different worldviews, and it makes unity in marriage difficult. In this case, it is important share your faith by your actions; don't try to fix, change or judge your spouse. Just love them. The rest is God's business. Pray for your spouse daily. Pray for his/her salvation. Pray that God would help you to love him/her selflessly. Pray that God would give you strength, grace, and encouragement on those days when you feel alone in your marriage.

- **If your marriage is struggling, get help.** Your parish can help connect you to Christian counseling centers or to Retrouvaille, which is an apostolate for troubled marriages. If you are in an abusive marriage, get help to enter into a process for addressing the abuse and any safety concerns.

For those of you who are struggling with divorce or a broken relationship it does not mean that you are less spiritual or less committed to marriage and family. Many have done all they could to save their marriages. Sometimes when a person is freed from a dysfunctional marriage, his/her relationship with God blossoms. Those who are divorced may take comfort in the story of Jesus and the Samaritan Woman at the Well (John 4:4-42). This poor woman had been married five times and was now living with yet another man. She had a lot of failed relationships in her past! However, Jesus' tenderness toward her and his sympathy for her situation is apparent. He offers this divorcée "living water," himself, which was what she had been searching for in all her relationships.

If you are a single parent for any other reason, know that you are not alone. Jesus is with you. While you can't be both a mother and father, you can still teach your children about Jesus and be an example by living your life in a holy and virtuous way. God knows that your family deals with many other pressures and problems that a nuclear family does not have to face. God also knows that you can feel overwhelmed by the responsibility of caring for your kids, maintaining a job, and keeping up with the bills.

You can also breathe a sigh of relief by remembering that over the course of your children's lives, God will send numerous people into their path to build on the work you have done at home. Ultimately, the Holy Spirit is the agent of conversion. This is true regardless of whether you are single, married, divorced, or widowed. Our job as parents is to simply create an environment in our home where Christ can be encountered and then we need to leave the rest to Jesus. You don't have to be the perfect parent in order to lead your family in becoming more Christ-like. Know that God gives particular graces to those who are experiencing hardships. In addition, it may be helpful to seek the fellowship of others who are in a similar situation as you and have similar goals to raise their kids in the faith. Support from friends, other family members and the church can help too.

A Christ-Centered Home

The Church summons Catholic families, in all their shapes and forms, to be a stable, loving and holy environment where Christ can be encountered. The catechetical programs that take place at parishes and Catholic schools are incredibly important, but a few hours a week in a catechism class isn't nearly enough for children to connect to Jesus. If you want your children to have strong faith that lasts, you need to nurture it at home by making Christ the center of your family. Faith is like a language—it is impossible to master by attending classes. It is more caught than taught. It is a tradition that is handed on from one generation to another, but one that the new generation must live in and pick up, as it were, through osmosis. The family is the first and best opportunity for this to take place. When it comes to more explicit learning, children are most teachable at the moment when they are curious and they have a question. These questions don't usually occur in a classroom setting, but often in the car on the way home from a friends' house. Parents are the primary evangelizers as well as the primary catechists of their children. Their role is absolutely irreplaceable. The role of fathers in particular is essential, since one of the greatest factors influencing a child's future practice of the faith is the religious involvement of his or her father. Amid all the pressure to prepare their children for success in life, parents need to realize that there is no greater success and no greater gift they can give their children than a relationship with Jesus and his Church, which endures throughout eternity.

So, what is a "Christ-centered home?" It's a place where family members speak and act and relate to one another in the awareness that Jesus himself is a participant in everything they do. How does this "Christ-centeredness" play itself out in the practical details of everyday life? To a certain extent it expresses itself differently from situation to situation. Every Christian family, like every Christian individual, is unique. But there are some common features we can expect to find in every genuinely Christ-centered home: it has joy, it is orderly, it is marked by grace, it is a place of service and a place where spiritual disciplines are practiced.

The following are some suggestions for introducing your child to Jesus and keeping him at the center of your home life.

- **Cover your family in prayer.** Prayer has the power to dramatically shift the spiritual atmosphere in your home. The enemy loves when chaos, tension, anger, stress, and frustration enter into our families. Don't allow this dynamic to rule your home. Praying helps to restore peace and change perspectives. Pray for your spouse and each of your children by name each day. Bring the concrete circumstances of their lives into this prayer (e.g., friendships, school/work situations, decisions to be made). Pray for physical, spiritual, emotional, and psychological protection. The world is filled with many philosophies on how to live; pray that your children can discern what is true and according to God's law and what is not. The enemy would like nothing more than to lure our children away from God, but we don't have to let him win. By virtue of our baptism, we can take authority over these spiritual battles.

- **Use the name of Jesus.** Talk about Jesus like you would any good friend. Tell your children when a prayer is answered or when you feel inspired by the Holy Spirit to do something. Incorporate Jesus into daily conversation. For example, when you say, "I love you" you can remind your child that Jesus loves him or her too. When you've lost something, let your children hear you pray to Jesus to help you find it. When your children are fascinated by the landscape, the weather, an animal, or anything else in nature, remind them that God is the creator of it all. When your children are afraid of something, point them to Jesus. Remind them God encourages us to fear not 365 times in the Bible, one for each day of the year. If you hear a siren or know someone who is sick, include this in your prayer at dinner time.

- **Teach your children to pray.** In addition to teaching your children rote prayers, encourage them to talk to Jesus in their own words about the things that are most important to them, and remind them to listen to what Jesus says back. Jesus desires to speak to our children, for them to know him, and follow his voice. Children have a natural capacity for God. They are open and trusting; they don't judge or get suspicious as adults do. As parents, we can help our children hear and recognize God's voice when they are young, so that when they are older, his voice is familiar when life becomes more complicated. God speaks to us in a variety of ways: through dreams, through images in our minds, through a song or Scripture verse, or through a whisper in our heart.

- **Pray together as a family.** Prayer is the life-breath of a Christ-centered home. As the saying goes, "Families who pray together stay together." When you pray together, each member of the family learns what it means to be intimate with God. When you see answers to prayer, you experience his love and his presence in your daily lives.

Children need to see genuine faith lived out in their parents' lives. So let your children hear you bringing your needs and requests before the Lord. When they do, they'll get the idea that Jesus can be trusted to guide us through every situation we encounter in life. Family prayer also deepens interpersonal relationships. It encourages family members to become more sensitive to one another's feelings. If your family is new to this kind of thing, avoid the temptation to manipulate or push. Keep family prayer as light and casual as possible. Start by praying about your kids' achievements, accomplishments, and positive experiences. If a child doesn't want to participate, don't make a scene. Over time, your family will grow into the practice of family prayer. An easy place to begin is before meals at home. Use the meal prayer time to ask children if they have any prayer intentions and incorporate these into your prayer. As your family becomes more comfortable praying together, try praying the rosary, allowing children to take turns leading a decade.

- **Pray over your children.** Look for opportunities to bless and pray over your kids. Often we think of "blessing" as something that God does, but it is a normative practice that goes all the way back in our Judeo-Christian history. In blessing your children, you speak words that express that they have your favor. The words of affirmation and love will have a deep impact on them. Blessing a child involves laying hands on the child and speaking words of God's blessing over them. Here are some examples:

  — "Lord, thank you for the gift of Matt in our lives. Please bless his day at school. Give him wisdom in his school work and grace as he interacts with his friends. Fill him with your Spirit and help him to have a blessed day. Amen."

  — "Jesus, please help Nick today with his exam. Give him the gift of peace and the knowledge he needs to do well. Amen."

  — "Heavenly Father, I lift up Melissa to you and I ask you to fill her with your peace. In the name of Jesus, I ask that you bring healing into her heart for any harsh words that she has heard from her friends. Help her to know how precious she is in your eyes and how loved she is in our family. I ask this through Christ, our Lord. Amen."

- **Make reading the Bible normative in your household.** Read the Bible regularly to your small children and encourage older children to read on their own. Help them to know the big picture of the story of salvation in the old and new covenant. There are many good Catholic resources (searchable on the Internet) that can familiarize you with how this story unfolds and culminates in Jesus.

- **Consider the physical environment of your home.** Invite your pastor or deacon to come and bless your home. Blessing of a home involves prayer and sprinkling of holy water. By blessing your home, you are putting your family and house under God's protection. If a priest or deacon is not available, you can sprinkle holy water in the rooms of your home yourself. Also, consider having religious items on your walls or shelves. Religious items remind us of our identity as Catholic Christians and help to serve as a focal point for prayer. In addition, make sure your child has access to good Christian music, videos, and toys.

- **Serve together.** Consider getting together with other families and doing charitable work. Most charitable non-profit organizations welcome volunteers to help with sorting clothes, giving food to the needy, or cleaning up grounds. Kids love to serve and doing good for others. It is a great way to put faith into action and demonstrate that serving others naturally flows out of our life in Christ.

- **Go to confession together as a family.** Seeing parents receive the sacrament of Reconciliation is a powerful witness to God's love and mercy.

- **Take control over your family calendar.** As your children become involved in various activities, the demands of coaches, music teachers, and dance instructors can be overwhelming. Don't let sports and other activities take priority over your family's faith life. It's ok to say "no" to the coach in order to have balance in your family life.

- **Go to Mass each week.** Going to Mass with small children can be a challenge. It's hard to get everyone dressed. It's hard to get everyone there on time. It's hard to keep them quiet during Mass while juggling toys, diapers, and crayons while older parishioners give you an evil glare. However, it is important for children to be familiar with the culture of worship. There's value in small children seeing a bunch of grown-ups sing songs, be reverent, pray to God, and receive the Eucharist. They learn that God is big, holy and important and that Sunday is a holy and special day we honor him. As a parent of young children, sometimes Mass feels more like a sacrificial act—instead of a gift that you receive, it is a gift that you give! Here are a few things that can help your growing family better experience the liturgy:[2]

  — Sit near the front so that children can be more engaged in what is happening in the sanctuary.

  — Decide ahead of time with your spouse what you expect of your children. Do you expect them to sit nicely in the pew? Do you want him or her to sing the songs? Set goals for these behaviors and be patient, firm, and kind as you teach your children what's expected. If these goals are not achieved, don't be discouraged! There's always next week!

  — Making stepping out of the church as boring as possible. Rather than entertaining them with toys in the vestibule, take them to a quiet space and say, "Are you ready to go back in and hear the music or read your Bible?" Over time, they will realize that sitting in church is more enjoyable.

  — Help your children know what is going on during Mass. For example, you can say, "This is the part where we sing songs. God loves to hear us sing!" "Now we are reading from the Bible. These are God's words for us! Listen to what he wants to say in your heart!" "Look, everyone is putting money in the basket. This money is for God's work in the church!" During the Eucharistic prayer you can say, "Look, Jesus is in the bread and wine. He can't wait to feed his people so that they can have God's blessing and strength!"

---

[2] Jessica Smartt, "How to Introduce Your Child to Jesus," (Melinda Martin, 2014): Chapter 4.

— Invite children to bring a journal to Mass and encourage them to listen to what God wants to say to them through the readings, prayers, homily or the Eucharist. Children who are too young to write can draw pictures of what they experience. This encourages active listening and participation in Mass and serves as good conversation on the way home.
— Celebrate Sunday by going out to eat after Mass or doing fun activities as a family. Try to get chores done before Sunday so that the Lord's Day can be a true day of rest and time for family.
— Take advantage of children's programs in your parish community such as Vacation Bible School, faith formation, and camps.

Make no mistake about it—the faith life of your children depends on YOU! God has entrusted them to you to lay the foundation for their adult life. The gun has fired and the race is on. Are you ready? Are you moving or standing still? Are you running aimlessly or staying in your lane? Don't forget that God has your back and will give you the grace for the journey and help you keep your eyes on the prize!

St. Paul offers some words of encouragement that piggy back on our relay race theme:

> Do you not know that the runners in the stadium all run in the race, but only one wins the prize? Run so as to win. Every athlete exercises discipline in every way. They do it to win a perishable crown, but we an imperishable one. Thus I do not run aimlessly; I do not fight as if I were shadowboxing. No, I drive my body and train it, for fear that, after having preached to others, I myself should be disqualified. (1 Corinthians 9:24-27)

I pray that the reflections and suggestions in this book are helpful to you and your family and the Lord blesses and anoints you in all your efforts. Please join me in this closing prayer:

Come Holy Spirit, fill the hearts of your faithful and kindle in them the fire of your love. Send forth your Spirit and they shall be created. And You shall renew the face of the earth.

O, God, who by the light of the Holy Spirit, did instruct the hearts of the faithful, grant that by the same Holy Spirit we may be truly wise and ever enjoy His consolations, Through Christ Our Lord, Amen.

Questions for Individual Reflection or Small Group Discussion

1. What strikes you about the passage in 2 Timothy?
2. Consider your own relationship with Jesus. What is one thing you can do to strengthen your relationship with him?
3. Consider the dynamic of your family life. What are some things you can do to make home more Christ-centered?

Bibliography

Archbishop Allen H. Vigneron. *Unleash the Gospel*, Detroit, MI: 2017.

Catholic Church. *Catechism of the Catholic Church*, 2nd ed. Washington, DC: USCCB, 2016.

Focus on the Family. "Beginning to Pray Together" Accessed August 1, 2019. https://www.focusonthefamily.com/marriage/growing-together-spiritually/spiritual-intimacy/beginning-to-pray-together.

Focus on the Family. "My Success as a Single Mom." Accessed August 1, 2019. https://www.focusonthefamily.com/lifechallenges/relationship-challenges/divorce/my-success-as-a-single-mom.

Franciscan Media. "Seven Things Catholics Should Know About Divorce." Accessed August 5, 2019. https://www.franciscanmedia.org/seven-things-catholics-should-know-about-divorce/.

Marriage Today. "My Spouse Isn't a Believer." Accessed August 4, 2019. https://marriagetoday.com/marriagehelp/spouse-isnt-believer/.

Smartt, Jessica. How to Introduce Your Child to Jesus. Melinda Martin, 2014.

The New American Bible Revised Edition. Washington, DC: Confraternity of Christian Doctrine, 2010. http://www.usccb.org/bible/.

Who was Jesus? Video. Bluefish TV. 2011.

Also Available by Anita Houghton

Kerygma 4 Kids—Grade School Edition

Kerygma 4 Kids Grade School Edition is an evangelization tool for children that proclaims the Good News of Jesus Christ in a unique and engaging way.

- helps children discover God's personal love for them
- includes guided meditations on Sacred Scripture to help children encounter the risen Christ
- presents an age-appropriate proclamation of the kerygma—the Good News of Christ's salvific work
- includes animated videos and engaging activities that reinforce the Gospel message
- includes an invitation to open their hearts to a personal friendship with Jesus Christ
- provides the language to help children share the Good News with others

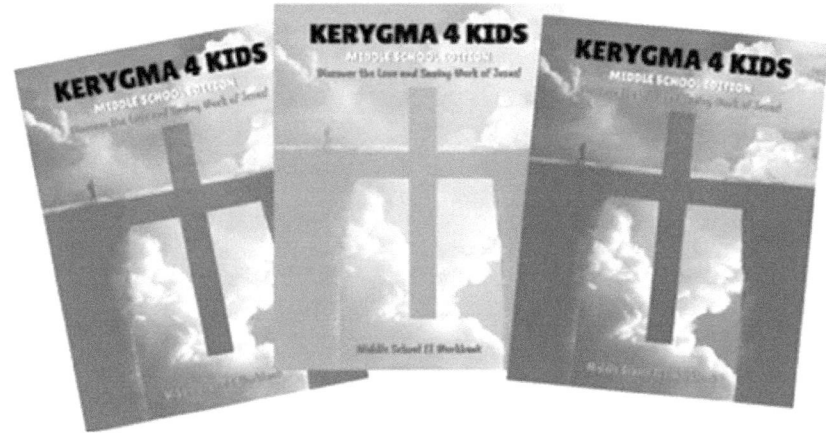

Kerygma 4 Kids—Middle School Edition

Kerygma 4 Kids Middle School Edition is a series of dynamic evangelization lessons for youth grades 6 through 8. Middle School years are a pivotal time for young people, during which they face numerous changes and challenges. These lessons connect the Gospel of Jesus Christ to the lives of Middle School youth.

- helps youth discover God's personal love for them
- includes guided meditations on Sacred Scripture to help youth encounter the risen Christ
- includes whiteboard animated videos and engaging activities that reinforce the Gospel message
- includes an invitation to open their hearts to a personal friendship with Jesus Christ
- provides the language to help them share the Good News with others

Purchase the complete set or individual lessons.
Visit www.ministry23.com/kerygma-4-kids
To order, call OSV at (800) 348-2440